Songs for the Earth

Songs for the Earth

Dear Yvonne + Roman
Hope you enjoy this?
Come to Vermont Sometime
Love
Len

Leonard Gibbs

Library of Congress Control Number:		2008911754
ISBN:	Hardcover	978-1-4363-9607-3
	Softcover	978-1-4363-9606-6

To order additional copies of this book, contact:
Xlibris Corporation
1-888-795-4274
www.Xlibris.com
Orders@Xlibris.com
57131

Contents

Introduction

Everything is One . . . no disconnects;
The Poet, and everything that surrounds the Poet.
All that is not the Poet's mind
      Is the Earth, the Universe.

In the Poet's mind is the Poet's life.
      All that the Poet has seen, smelled, touched, felt, tasted,
      And all that the Poet has ever loved.

The Poet and the Earth, the Universe
      Speak to each other . . . listen!
The Earth, the Universe give pen and paper,
      Sand and stone.

The Poet gives back words, songs, poetry.
Praises the Earth, the Universe, and the Listeners,

And the Mother.

About the Rain

I've made extensive studies of the rain.
Rain's not just water dropping from a cloud.
Each drop has lived a thousand lives, has been
a part of oceans, rivers, puddles, streams.

I have been trapped in rain on mountain hikes,
hiding beneath the overhanging crags,
and washed in April's baths, and reveled in
the summer storms that swept across the Lake.

And once I saw the rain, with heavy drops
march down the dusty road to end a drought
while I stood in the sun, and waited, glad
to be one with the rain, its majesty.

This is the Mother's blood, this gentle rain,
shed for the earth, to let it live again.

Alpha Dog

Ellie's the alpha dog, West Highland White
(chosen to match one color of my scotch.)
The other one is black. as black as night,
a pair of terriers and a joy to watch.

Ellie, as alpha dog, is not too smart;
her time responding is unusually slow.
She waits for Flora's signal when to start
her barking for her breakfast, even though

she sees me open up the pantry door
to get the kibbles that she knows are there;
we fear her vision's rather poor,
but she responds when Evo's in the air.

The duties of the alpha dog are small;
nap on the sofa, wait for Flora's call.

Always, the Night

The moon has set, the sun has not yet come;
the dark before the dawn, the morning watch
when all the dreads of all the dreams of night
are fading, and the hopes of day return.

I've shared the darkness of this watch at sea,
seen the sun rising, seen it spread its light
across the ocean, set the sea afire,
deny the night once more, and yet have known

the daylight watches are a transient gift;
the day is passing fair, but night will come,
the earth-created shadow of the sun
denies the momentary joy of day.

There is the fantasy, the cheerful light,
and the reality, the dark of night.

Another Universe of Crows

The crows are a dark beauty, fill the land,
scouring the fallow fields for bits of corn,
lords of the seaweed, taking as their due
the ocean's offering to these black-robed priests.

They fly at my approach, but never far
as if I were the unbelonging one,
intruder in their world, to be ignored
or coolly watched until I go away.

They sing a single word, libretto brief
atonal, raucous, in another tongue,
a monstrous sound, impersonal and hard
strange visitors of foreign time and space.

Theirs is a song that tells creation end.
Some messengers a savage god would send.

Appalachian Spring

Rose red darkness
morning=s come,
May morning,
sunset turned around.

Slow mists rising
through the balsam;
rhododendron dropping
dew on the ground.

Soft sound of sunlight
rippling over ridges,
calling up a bird to sing
a new world found.

At the Bird Feeder

They come at dawn, the spirit-birds,
here and not here and here again,
awakened now from their cold sleep,
lacing the frozen world together.

Fast-flitting chickadees,
belligerent nut-hatch, single sparrow,
a downy woodpecker and
gold and purple finches in bobbing flight.

These are the small gifts of winter,
prayers in motion
over the motionless snow
among the black trees.

Autumn Sadness

When all the leaves are fallen,
when all the trees are bare,
and when the evening chill
has blown the mists away
and naked stars burn
and the moons of harvests
glow on dead shocks and dying vines,

Autumn is a painted coffin;
red and gold skin on the skull.
Beauty's betrayal
lies under loveliness.

Falling leaves are dreadful things,
building bridges across the sad valleys
of the end of summer
to shores of dying hope.

Balance of the Earth

We have made deserts where the flowers grew
and built lush gardens spots to feed our eyes.
We paved the fertile fields so we could fly
hither and yon when sitting still would do.

We've had enough to eat, and have grown large;
across the world, across the town, they starve.
We curse the peaceful, say they only serve
who kill for glory, wage unending war.

We have thrown off the balance of the earth.
We could have loved, and sung; found poetry
for all our needs, and made our sharing free,
made wondrous futures start at every birth.

We have our reason; everything to gain.
Return to Eden; build the earth again.

Beyond the Trees

Beyond the trees, the valley.
Beyond the valley, green hills
the piedmont, the tidewater, the ocean.
Beyond the ocean, the stars.

I am here, flesh stranded
essentially immobile
in my watchtower.

But my angel goes where it will,
and though my voice is cracked with age
and too much shouting

my angel sings
the arias of the universe;

my sunlight shines
above the clouds of doubt.

Bluets

The bluets come to say that winter's gone.
These tiny flowers carpet under shrubs
in pleasant shadows, never one alone,
a multitude of blossoms near the curb

of walkways in the slowly waking earth,
color where there no color was, beside
the cold gray-brown of winter's frozen hearth.
They mark the start of summer's rising tides.

I walk among these tiny flowers, and pray
a prayer of thanks that summer does not end;
it only rests, that in the lengthening day
the bluets bloom, and in that instant blend

the past and future as I walk between
them in the present winter-ending scene.

The Burden of the World

The flowers bear the burden of the world.
Under the delicate blossoms lie the steel,
the earth's supporting structure, the real hope
of the rebirth of beauty in the spring.

The fading flowers of autumn are the wreath
of funeral sadness, final breath
lost in the rattle of the falling leaves,
the wilting aster, gloomy song of death.

The greening earth is pleasant, and the bright
yellow of willows, blue of distant hills
unfold a canvas ready for the light,
but these alone will not hold back the night.

There must be flowers, bright in morning dew.
There must be flowers, nothing else will do.

Butterfly Mysteries

I

Everyone knows that if a butterfly
flaps its wings in Los Angeles,
the effect will be felt in Boston,
a gentle zephyr grown into a nor'easter.
What everyone doesn't know
is what might happen
if two butterflies
flap simultaneously
In Los Angeles.

II

Am I a butterfly
dreaming that I am a man,
or am I a man dreaming
that I am a butterfly
dreaming that I am a man?
Or am I a
a slightly tipsy Zen poet?

III

Butterflies are famous
for taking up residence in human stomachs
before important events.
No one seems to know
what particular species of butterfly
is symbiotic with us,
or where they go
when we relax.

IV

When this poets eyes are tired
and floaters and golden sparks
flutter across his visual field,
he sometimes thinks of butterflies.
Strange that all that beauty
can be such a nuisance.

V

Butterflies do not eat butter,
nor do they breed in butter.
They do not hatch from butter
as fruit flies hatch from peaches.
They do fly,
so their name is half correct
which is not bad
for a frittilarinarianist.

VI

The prize fighter,
when he is knocked out,
sometimes sees butterflies
and sometimes stars
as he falls,
thus two great beauties of the universe
as he drifts toward darkness.

VII

After a whiff of cyanide
the butterfly is pinned on cork,
carefully through the thorax
so as not to disturb
the delicate scales of color
the collector hopes to freeze,
which, of course,
can never be frozen.

VIII

We wonder why the Monarch
flies two thousand miles to Mexico;
a simple ancestral memory?
A need to stretch its wings after a summer of frittering?
A family reunion with cousins from Peru
A surrender to the travel agent's slight exaggeration?
This much is sure; no butterfly
in his or her right mind
would stay for a Vermont winter.

IX

Snowflake Bentley photographed,
for the record,
five hundred snowflakes,
and concluded,
"no two snowflakes are alike"

His sample, 500
out of 3.8×10^{23} flakes/snowfall,
is suspiciously small
to give credence to his conclusion

But, I feel the same way about butterflies, and I don't have
even one
photograph.

The Cavern

With half my brain
      I revel in the facts the guide
      with his faked enthusiasm
      in the tenth tour of his shift is giving us.

"it took a hundred million years for water
      drop by drop
      to carve away this pit, and then
      to build these columns you see here.

Then he turns off the lights.
      "This is real darkness,
      here three-hundred feet below the surface.
      No sunlight ever reaches here"

I find the gee-whiz science of the interpreter
      interesting, but of a school-boy nature;
      material for his term paper in the fall.

What does he know of caverns?
      He spouts some superficial facts
      while darkness calls from the stones.

This is the abyss, known only to the agéd soul.
      True darkness.
      Only the stones, and God
      know the absence of light,
      know emptiness.

The Circle

How warm the blanket is, the crusted snow
that guards the tiny beasts that sleep below
in drowsy waiting, 'til the sun shall beam
and heat the frozen world, and end the dream

that passed the nameless time among the roots
that furnished winter sustenance, and shoots
of vegetables they stored against the fast,
knowing that spring would truly come, at last.

The March winds came, and blew away the frost
and April came, and gardeners dug and tossed
the fertile earth to help the seeds to grow
to furnish food before the coming snow

when all the little animals shall keep
warm under crusted snow, their winter sleep.

Cloud Cover

Under clouds
leaves might be green
but trees are hidden.
I am not allowed this knowledge.

Under clouds
blue periwinkle
might carpet the woods-floor
but in the mist flowers are invisible.
I am not allowed this knowledge.

Above clouds, sun
or moon or stars;
there might even be God.
I am not allowed this knowledge.

Clouds on Dead Creek

Low lying clouds on Dead Creek, the summer's
painting, a soft patina, morning's glow,
a blinding light announces day has come.
Away my spirit, let the poems flow.

This is the puzzle, how it comes about
that clouds and light and all the space between
wake in my mind connections to without
and call up words that let me praise the scene.

Where is my being? Is it in my mind,
or in the world surrounding me, or both?
What is the secret of the joy I find
in reveling in visions? I am loathe

to separate myself from things around.
I trust all worlds are one, all things are bound.

Cold Spring in Vermont

The days are true, the nights prevaricate;
cats coiled in nodes of warmth sleep in the hay.
The green is stunted, willows hesitate,
and glorious flowers shiver for the day.

Dark curtained sunrise's slow to share its light.
Winter is playing hide and seek with Spring.
The days are warmer, colder still the nights;
the aged stagehand will not pull the string.

The earth has come full circle round the sun
bringing the springtime for the season's show,
but timid actors do not trust the run.
They do not want to tread the boards in snow.

The audience is eager, yet it's clear:
the globe is warming, everywhere but here.

The Columbine

They may be tiny, but they are not small.
Ask any elf, the ones that monitor
life in the garden, guard the dreams of spring,
keep warm the seeds; the Columbine's a giant.

The elfin flowers of the Columbine
surprise me in my garden's shaded spots,
from under Peonies they leap, show forth
behind the leafy spikes of Daffodils.

They're trumpets in the orchestra of flowers
with clear, sweet piping tones that float above
into the place of angels, gently move
from earth to empty space among the stars,

What in this universe may we call small?
Each part is mighty; being here is all.

Contrail at Sunrise

Sunrise today's no casual event;
a splash of cloudy lightning starts the day,
contrail misshapen, ripped by winds aloft,
red vapors coalescing mark their path.

No doubt commuters early, half-asleep,
these travelers did not mean to leave it there
trailing the prismed raindrops as they fly,
dragging the scar they make across the sky.

We have no credit here, except perhaps
by making the machines we are the cause
of accidental beauty, joy unplanned,
the chance for angels' brushes, heaven's hand.

We lift out art as humble offerings.
True beauty flies aloft on angels' wings.

The Crow at Worldrise

At the beginning of the world
by which I mean the larger world,
the universe, the whirling galaxies,
pulsars, red giants, white dwarfs, worm holes,
planetary systems held apart by light years,
and all the other parts of this endless
but not limitless lot of cluttered space
of which we are the center,

At the beginning of the world,
at the time of the big bang,
which was itself before the beginning,
or just after, when creation was casting
red shadows across Magellanic clouds
and the emptiness began to be filled
with firmaments and nights and days,

In the beginning, when the first light came
to the young earth,
the first sound, after the big bang, of course,
was the voice of a crow calling across the world.

And, I believe, when all this roiling universe
has run down hill,
when all its parts lie without energy,
limp on an even plain,
there will be a crow, one black bird,
giving its raucous benediction.

The Daffodil

They bloom in many colors, daffodils;
yellow and gold, red, orange, even pink;
bi-colored trumpets, ruffled-edged display
varieties of joy, just for a day.

They are the flowers of the early spring;
with crocuses they rise, and bravely bring
their celebration through the melting snow,
prevail against the later storms and show

a contradiction of the common truth,
that flowers only bloom in summer warmth.
They always bless us with this fine surprise,
a splendid sight to over-wintered eyes.

The spring begins with daffodils so bold.
Thanks to the Mother for this child of gold.

Damn Old Copernicus

Damn old Copernicus
for proving that the earth
is not the center of the universe,
for stealing our moment of glory.

But he was wrong, of course.
We all know that anywhere
in this vast expanse that glows
with memory of the great primal bang
can be the center.

That aside,
the earth, indeed, is center after all.
This is the place you go from, if you go,
and this is where you will arrive
when your trip is done.

The Dandelion

Behold the noble dandelion in spring;
so quick to open, suddenly in sight.
Brown fields, now greening, overnight display
these golden specks that open with the day.

"Tooth of the Lion", referring to the leaf,
a jagged dagger threatening at first glance,
yet in the irony of nature's gifts
an edible and quite delicious plant.

And just as quickly blossoms disappears,
leaving the crown of feathered fruits to fly
across the fields, to keep their kind alive,
and from one flower spring a thousand more.

Some call this little plant a noxious weed.
I see the world turn golden from its seed.

The Darkness

From enormous darkness
God comes in small, flickering fires;
fox-fire, will o' the wisp,
sheet lightning on the undersides of clouds,
fire flies on an August night;
even stars and galaxies are tiny bits of light.
God wears a blessed veil,
protects our souls' dim eyes
against his glory.
Praise darkness now!

A Day of Spring

A day of spring, with lilacs in the air,
we floated without being, purely there.
You felt it, you beside me I will swear,
yet each alone was blessed, each had a share.

There was an almost cloudless sky above.
A gentle breeze made new born leaflets move.
We heard the music of the mourning dove.
We knew that what created this was love.

The springtime locust snow began to fall.
We saw the ivy freshening on the wall.
Flowers and fields we saw; we heard the call
of distant crows and cattle, large and small.

In memory this spring day has always stood.
Did we dream this one day, or was it God?

Despairing Gray

The Vermont sky is a despairing gray,
portends some rain or snow, A cloudy day
is usual in this fog-begotten state;
if we want sun we usually have to wait.

Those who have a cash and time now all go south
leaving the winter to the poor, and youth
who're trapped in education's savage toils,
who use the dull gray ski-slopes as their foils

against the numbing cold and muted sky
of winter, and in summer hear the cry
of farmers praying for the rain to fall
to irrigate the corn crops, which is all

the Vermont sky will nourish in this day
of everlasting, all-despairing gray.

Dog From Space

Flora, I swear, has come from outer space
with brows like John L. Lewis, and with eyes
reflecting knowledge far beyond her race
she stares with wisdom from her fireside place.

Now, dogs are sometimes smart and sometimes dumb.
We have one, Ellie, who is sweet as pie,
but she'd get lost in her own kennel if
we closed the door behind her in the dark.

Flora knows when we're happy or when not.
Her only problem, she's inclined to bark
to cheer us up, which doesn't help a lot.
But Flora tries. She always is our spark.

It's strange, but I am sure a wisdom lies
in that small head, behind those glowing eyes.

The Earth's Our Friend

The earth's our friend; we are not always hers.
We live as strangers come to a strange land.
We come to conquer, dodge her welcome hand,
make gardens into deserts, bring our wars.

Our Mother's given us a gentle touch
to till the fields, plant gardens, tend the trees;
Eden was there for us, and still could be
if we could rest, relax our savage rush

to reach the stars, which to our brilliant minds
give hope that some new home is waiting there.
Our earth's a staging site, not near so fair,
an arid place we dream to leave behind.

But space is God's play-place; it is not ours.
Our home is here, the Garden, not the stars

Empty Times

Maxwell and I lie in the morning sun
thinking of nothing, quite a bit of that.
There might be worries, and there might be fun
but not for now. He shows me how, my cat

to sit and stare in vacant thoughtlessness
beyond the empty windows, seeing naught;
blessed by the moment's total emptiness,
absent the process of creative thought,

not thinking of the unbeloved face
of deadly enemy or mouse escaping.
We ruminate about deep cosmic space
where nothing is, and nothing needs replacing.

We think tomorrow will be time enough
to worry about life and other stuff.

The Final Scene

Timeless. The suns rise not. The harvest moon
lies hid behind the eastern hills. The stars
are still. Polaris, pivot of the bears
creates no circles in the northern sky.

All waits. The breathless frozen universe
without the angels' songs, it's echoes lost;
the praising chorus silent, with no change.
Celestial motion stopped, the galaxies

float quietly in stasis, balanced now,
the pinpoint of eternity their rest.
There is no motion, nor will ever be.
Creation's done; the cosmos is at peace.

From the first word, beginning's awful power
"til now, when time has found it's final hour.

Gloom

The sun is shining, so where is the joy
I should be feeling when I wake to see
the shrouded mountains at my valley's edge
and blue, reluctant, between heavy clouds?

I do not celebrate the hinted hope
that the storm looming will not break.
A touch of sunlight's not a sunny day;
only a cloudless sky will pave the way

for celebration of my spirit's need
for light, and proper light at that;
not a world lit by misty colored gloom
that sifts through vaporous cracks into my room.

I'll go to bed, and close my eyes again
outwait the thunder and the pounding rain.

The Goldfinch

Gold is the marker of our wealth, we hoard
the shiny metal for our rainy days.
But there's more gold than we can hide away;
the gold of flowers and birds cannot be stored.

The Goldfinch comes in mufti, travel kit,
then quickly throws his winter cape away,
becomes the lightning of the summer day,
erratic flight, a bouncing glide and flit.

The golden fields, the early dandelions,
the daffodils, goldfinches, all have come
to splash their gold against the Vermont gray,
bright life unceasing, lightening the day.

The Goldfinch is a song that we have heard
and gloried in, a necessary bird.

Gull Poetry

There's sorcery of sight here on the beach
and I, with an affinity for light
see diamonds on a fractured sea of jade.
The gull that glides above this broken plain
can only see, I think, some simple grays
and underneath those grays a hope for food.

Inseparate from sea and sky and sand,
poised for the treacherous moment that reveals
his food, he waits in elemental greed.
His thoughts, perhaps not even thoughts, that flit
in the dark and tiny caverns of his brain
connect the world in one harmonious meal.

But I, more noble, with this luminous mind
connected to a universal light,
seek all my nourishment in perfect words.
And if I dive, as he, into the sea
I only act for inspiration's sake
to find a line to sing the oceans power.

With this gull spirit, mine, my mind would soar
and write a poem that creates a world.
But words, as feet, are sand bound, finally,
while he dives, kills and eats, squawks and circles up
to drift above time-frozen sand and sea.
He mindless waits, and is the poetry.

A Hawk Waits

Nature will be balanced, life and death
walk hand in hand, across the fertile earth.
The predator and prey in partnership
complete the circle, and refresh the land.

The hawk that circles high above the mouse
is hungry, sees the little beast, and dives.
The mouse, in his quick foolish hunt for food
becomes the meal, fills out his destiny.

The hawk in time will die, the majesty
of flight that let him soar above the fields
will end in one last plummet, as he yields
his savage spirit to the worms below.

The earth is just; mindless necessity
lets all be born, insists that all must die.

High Moment

We often wake in evil times, and fall
into the deep recesses of our souls,
are uninspired in Nature's gloomy pall
as day by day the distant thunder rolls.

But in a sudden clash of dark and light
the sun escapes the prison of the clouds
and suddenly our spirits rise to flight
pushing aside our self-defeating shrouds.

And in that moment of our Mother's grace
the universe is set ablaze and we
stand blest and naked in her glorious face,
a momentary joy, an instant free.

We wait on darkened mountain-tops to see
the risen sun . . . to glimpse eternity.

High Noon

High Noon. The sundial has no shadow now.
Time waits, a pause; the center of the day;
the earth has stopped its spin. The new moon shows
its mirror side unmoving in the sky.

Birds are at rest. The soaring hawks descend
to wait on dead limbs in the stone-still trees.
There are no sounds, no cricket-voice to lend
life to the quiet day, no buzzing bees.

It cannot last. This stillness will not stay;
peace for a moment at sun's apogee . . .
one instant silent, soft, and then the day
begins to move . . . the world again is free.

This was the still-point of the turning earth.
The moment of the universe's birth.

Hot winds of August

The seasons come to this, at summers end,
when aster's blossoms fade and fall to dust.
The hot winds blow, and the tall grasses bend
and golden birds-foot trefoil turn to rust.

Our days are breathless, heavy in the heat
of August's sun, an unrelenting fire
burning the empty fields, the stubbled wheat,
the scars of harvest, a thread-bare attire.

The air is thick with floating angel seeds,
the tiny parachutes that promise life
remains, wild flowers and the roadside weeds
to last against the winter's coming strife.

This is the time between, the waiting earth.
The end of summer calls; prepare the hearth.

Iced in for Winter

Iced in for winter, soul a sheltered lake,
a broad expanse of cold and white, nothing
below, no depth, no warm inversion stored
to let the resting life return in spring.

From here, the winter days stretch out beyond
my hopeful vision; earth's a frozen pond.
Oh, I could skate, walk on the ice, admire
the stark cold beauty, or I could aspire

to write hot poetry in fiery tones,
thrown out to bring the sun, deny the cold;
but no, my spirit's matchless, cold my bones.
There is no thaw in sight. Winter's on hold.

This happens every year around this time.
The muse has left no music; only rhyme.

Invasive Species

"Invasive Species", they complain at length.
Vermont aristocrats must keep it pure.
the way things were before those from away
began to creep into this pristine state.

I'm one of those who came here from the south,
seen as invader, too, I'm pretty sure.
I may or may not be allowed to stay.
My welcome here is cool, at any rate.

Virginia loosestrife, possums here in strength,
coyotes have come hunting at the lure
of native sheep or chickens, so they say,
all foreigners the natives still berate.

The motto here is that we will not change,
invasive species must get off the range.

It's April

It's April, and the geese are flying south
against the evidence of memory;
this time of year they should be flying north
to scavenge sister Canada's largesse.

And through my kitchen window I've observed
the sun has traveled too far north this year,
already rising over Mansfield's peaks
beyond its normal limits, so I fear

it's broken from its orbit round the world,
changing the symmetry of Heaven and Earth;
with gravity awry, we could be hurled
into eternal winter, endless night.

The season's out of joint; that much is clear,
and no one wants the job to make it right.

Landsman's Lament

I do not love the ocean very well.
It seems the enemy, and calls to me
not for my love, but to complete the brotherhood
of sailors drowned through all the time
they've tried to use it,
or to conquer it, and failed.

It has its fascination, true enough;
that I am weightless when I swim,
and close to flying in the warm
clear waters of the coral reefs.
And I am tempted, when the wind is up,
to put my sail against the waves
and test my strength against its demons;
but only tempted.
I like it better on the beach, alive.

I am no friend of men-o'-war and sharks,
Of jagged stones and seaweed slime,
of towering blasts of surf against the rocks,
of vicious, twisting breakers
or of all the overpowering things
the ocean is.

I love the fools who rush
to ride the raging waves,
the warriors of the day.
I love them and will weep when they are gone,
when their wild voices mix
with all the voices of the drowned
I hear in the undertones
of the constant murmur of the sea.

I wait upon the beach, and watch
and think; someone must still be here
to sing the warriors tales,
someone who knows enough to fear
and sing the ocean that he does not love.

The Last Leaf

When the snow has finally clothed the land
and shadows of the wind set off the white,
with shadows of bare trees and jutting stones,
when gray-cloud winter now has claimed to

define all beauty we shall see until
the northing sun returns to melt the ice
and lets the streams begin to run again
and gentle winds of April wake the flowers;

until that blessed time there is one leaf
left hanging on the maple near our door,
a leaf the russet autumn left behind,
a scarlet leaf, one spot against the white

of winter, color of our hope and blood,
life held above the cold of winter's flood.

Life Cycles

What differences the times of life shall make.
Born helpless, sucking babe in mother's arms,
soon crawling, walking, running in the wake
of elders who will protect us from harm.

Then from the shadows of the wiser ones,
exploring worlds of nature and of love,
a traveler loosed from all parental homes
a warrior, businessman, then one to strive

against the tide of passion to create
a solid world for those who follow him.
Then age, time of reflection, time to wait
in restful patience, prisoner to the whim

of those who care for old and dying men,
closing the cycles in a blessed end.

Lilacs

Lilac, the royal flower. Queen of May,
spreading her scent, angelic breath of Heaven,
her perfume hovers everywhere we go;
the smell of life, after the ice and snow.

But in the spring of life we are in death.
Lilacs remind us of our tragedies;
her flowers blossom, and the blossoms fall,
the rush of history that consumes us all.

Sad memories that will not disappear
hang in the purple cascade of her flowers.
Knowledge of loss, an unexpected tear
portray the end of love, the closing hours.

A flower of sadness and a flower of love;
bless beauty, lilac, as you bless the grave.

Lost Stars

Often, on cold and cloudless nights I see
stars the burned out a million years ago,
image of sourceless light, celestial show
that travels on throughout eternity.

We trust that bits of knowledge, spectral shifts
will let us know the history of a star;
but that is purely faith. It is too far
to travel out to see that primal rift

between star's birth and final blazing fire
that spent its fuel in a glorious end,
an act of death allowing it to send
the endless knowledge of its funeral pyre.

For all we know, the stars may all be dead
and we alone in universal dread

Maple Syrup

Cold mists are rising over the Dead Creek.
These chilly mornings mark the end of spring,
when warm days after cool nights will bring
the maple's juices rising to the taps.

The wood that over winter farmers sawed
and split to heat the sap, to thicken it
into sweet syrup that Vermonters love,
now ready for the furnace and the pans

where saps evaporate, and leave behind
this nectar of the gods, Olympians,
who live on our Green Mountains, well defined
as drinkers of the only stuff we tin.

We've heard that other states will counterfeit.
Be careful! Only Vermont made is it!

March

The playful lions of March are passing through,
thrashing the drying sheets that we hung out,
our flags that celebrate the end of old
King Winter's temporary, failing reign.

Kites bounce along the ground with broken tails,
chased by these mighty cats, who're out to steal
kites, hats, and sheets, or anything they've seen,
rip off the shingles, tear a broken screen.

These lions, invisible, will come and go,
there and not there, created by some whim
of waking warmth in fields now freed of snow,
warning the waiting world that Spring will come.

Gifted they were with transitory power,
but they will go, and leave the April shower.

Morning Sky, with Clouds

This is not poetry nor philosophy
Just a reflection on the morning sky, with clouds.

How many times have I seen the sunrise?
      Not more than days that I have waked.
How many colors can the human eye define?
      Seven, at least, or more than we can count.
How can the blaze of light on undersides of clouds
turn to dull slate blue, without warning?
      The angle of incidence of the sunlight
      changes quickly with the spinning world.
Where do the colors go?
      Nowhere. They were never there.

Today the sky will still be blue.
Clouds will be white, some lined with darkness.
Clouds will be only water, insubstantial mist,
      with shapes of herringbones or dragons.
Meteorologists will name the clouds,
      according to altitude, shape, size and function,
but they will still be floating vapor.

Clouds will pass by,
      not noticing the desert's need,
or they will stop, drop rain or snow,
      not noticing our desire.

Most Glorious Mountain

Most glorious, holy mountain, sacred grove,
no granite summit, but a stand of pine
with branches trimmed man-height, a floor of dust;
beyond an altar stone, the endless hills.

This temple smells of sacrifice, of blood.
Beelzebul, lord of the flies, was here,
or Pan, the earth's goat-footed troubadour
who pipes to dance the funeral minuet.

I did not worship here, though I was called.
I felt the presence of the ancient gods.
I pray the God of Light deliver me;
protect me from that darkness and that joy.

For I would go again, perhaps to stay,
to love the haunted night, forsake the day.

Mountain Sunrise

It's wonderful how I can flick the sun
around the sky by dashing to and fro
from ridge to dell! Oh, I can make him run
among the trees; I simply walk along.

And once I made the sun set in the north,
almost, but then his latitude was wrong.
You understand, this can't be done at night,
and there must be at least one hill in sight,

but given proper silhouettes, and dusk
and dawn, I move from dark to light at will;
I make the game. I am Apollo here.
It will be sunset soon? My chariot down?

Oh well. We have a thousand mornings still.
The night has come? Why then, I'll move the moon.

Naked Beauty

I loved her naked beauty best of all,
walked in her angry surf and on her sand,
talked with the seals that came to call
to bring their wisdom from a distant land.

Climbed every hill, breathed in her mountain's breath,
bathed in the autumn leaves in falling showers,
entwined myself in all her warp and weft,
reveled from sunrise through the running hours.

All of my gifts were hers, I took from her
the riches of my blood, my very life,
her mysteries uncountable that were
the joys of growing and the joy of strife.

The only gift the Mother did not give;
the gift of endless time in which to live.

The Night is Ending

The night is ending; now my sleep is done,
the first dim lights of morning sweeping through,
freeing the stars. The moon has set, the Sun
prepares a canvas washed in lightest blue.

Sunrise is soft, its muted colors flow
across a faded sky, like thoughts that come
and drift away as ending nights disclose
the duties if the day, to stay or roam

across the wondrous world in search of joy;
of Eden's beauty just before the fall,
of Homer's music round the siege of Troy,
or of the Freedom at the fallen wall,

or of the many places I might be,
as waking opens up eternity.

No Scraps

This piece of wood was meant to be a part
of some new home, or restful rocking chair.
It came up short, a failed utility,
not good for houses or for furniture.

But nothing will be wasted on the earth;
at least it can decay and be a part
of the substrate, or feed the hearth
with fire, give pleasure to a weary heart.

All will return. The past's the present now
and will become the future in its time.
The earth is self-contained. The Mother's plow
will turn this soil of stars from which she grew.

There are no scraps. Each tiny piece of wood
sustains the universe, remains its food.

No Settled Rest

There is no settled rest for Maxwell cat.
Oh, surely he'll lie quietly in the sun
until he finds that we are somewhere else
he cannot get to, calls until we run

to open any door that's closed to him.
He'll scratch the threshold with his mighty claws,
demand a quick response to every whim,
and scratch and howl, keep howling without pause.

He doesn't ask for love; he wants respect
and services for every need he feels.
This cat's a savage; don't plan to collect
affection from his paws, or try to steal

a hug when Maxwell cat is passing by.
He will not pause for love . . . don't even try!

Occasional Sun

Now smile, you child of night. The sun is here.
Look at the colors, multi-shades of green.
Try being cheerful, give praise for the flowers;
rejoicing in these gifts, this rarer scene.

It's earths proclivity to rain each day.
(unless, of course, it is a time of drought)
It does no good to say "rain, go away;"
even when it does we know it's just about

to come again, So praise the sun for now;
don't grump because it does not always shine.
It's really there to make the flowers grow;
it's incidental gift of joy is fine.

Hang on, relax, go with old nature's flow.
Enjoy the sunlight, as we watch it go.

The Ocean's Edge: Letter One

This was my morning walk upon the beach
in early dawn, edged on my left
     by constant, murmuring surf
and on my right by rocks too large even
     for ocean waves to take away.

Some eastern clouds set off the rising light,
curtained the meeting of the sea and sky
and made for me a room,
     large enough to walk in,
yet not so large that I must be forever lost.

Contained; that was the word; a universe contained,
small enough to be a part of.
     Not like the night and stars
where I might fall from off the earth and
     into galaxies.

No. Morning on the beach, walking south,
     was manageable,
'til crowded by the rocks and tide
I was herded into the beach's end, and had to stop.
And now I turned, sea on my right, rocks on my left,
and turning met myself.

Well, only my footprints, really; I was still myself,
but walked into a collision with my past, thinking
　　　now I see this way, but then I was seeing that,
　　　then feeling the pleasure of the sunrise,
　　　but now how pebbles hurt my feet.
And I was the surf, curling on the beach of my own history,
　　　and for a moment I lost the safety of that room,
　　　and for a moment galaxies appeared
　　　unbounded now by stones, or sea, or clouds,
and for a moment I saw through my large
　　　and ancient history
as in the instant before I had seen my endless future,
and then the two collided and were still.

Footprints, then; only footprints,
　　　the ecstasy of terror gone,
I on the sand, between the seawall and the ocean's edge,
with the eastern sky fully draped,
and the path only the pathway home.

The Ocean's Edge: Letter Two

There are those scholars who can name
by species, color, range and habitat,
each kind of bird found on the sand and flats,
and who thereby, in nasal recitation of the facts,
have gained the ancient right that comes with naming;
they have dominion over all the birds (and beasts).

I find this dull.
Some birds I know because
by constant repetition facts are forced on me.,
to like or not to like.
But anyway, I know gulls, crows and cormorants;
I see and hear them constantly, gulls and crows more,
and cormorants less often, for if I've got it right
those are the dusky ones that spend
most of their working time submerged
in tidal swamps or brackish rivers after
food, or knowledge, or whatever they find there
in those dark waters, and the rest of the time
digesting, I suppose, what they have gained,
perched on high distant wires in gawky congregations.

And crows, don't be surprised,
come to the beach.
Like motorcycles, they are everywhere,
I think the raucous voice of crows
announced the first day of creation,
at noon, after the morning's glorious blast,
and will, I think,
cry out the benediction
in the vespers of the universe
And crows, to bring them back to earth, would just as soon
pick over piles of seaweed for small beasts
as search between the clods for wasted corn.

And what to say of gulls?
That they fly well,
that they can be quite still.
suspended on the wind,
and that they make a powerful third
to this trio that I know; gulls, crows and cormorants,
The gulls, for all their mindlessness,
add wondrous beauty to the scheme.

This dissertation on the birds that I can name
is only here to frame a further scene.
One day I saw, lit by the rising sun,
three tiny birds, not knee-high to a gull;
three birds all nameless, speckled brown
that walked with twittering steps to the water's edge
and stood accepting what the tidal rush brought in.

Smaller than gulls, or cormorants or crows,
smaller than robins (another bird I know),
they stood, and danced a bit, in elegant contempt
of the mighty sea they faced,
took what they wished, and twittered on their way.

So what is it we have?
There's Size, and Power, and overwhelming Strength,
and Noise, and Flight, and Numbers.
There are Reflection, Patience, Knowledge, real Dominion
and always Rhythm and sweet Beauty . . .
And these three tiny birds with twittering steps
moving among them all,
tweaking the ocean's edge with monstrous unconcern.

One Tree

Before the stars fell down that August night
Tree stood in placid beauty, as before;
perennial Tree, not older than the stars
but older far than me, a massive store

of life that framed the blazing universe,
Leonids flashing past unmoving limbs.
No breeze blew on the earth, but in the sky
a storm of burning meteors went by.

I have this Tree I watch, my single mark
of being here in transitory times.
The universe may burn, there's stars enough
to fuel all the changes I shall see.

But surely, when the falling star appears
the Tree's the lasting symbol of my years.

Our Eden

Swamp gases burning in the firmament,
celestial fire-flies, and St. Elmo's flame,
the hunter's beacons, furnaces of gods
the sailor's guide in the dark, dreadful night.

There was a time we prayed to heavenly sights,
kneeling in grateful terror to those lights,
but now with measurements of spectral shifts
we've done away with all the ancient myths.

With simple calculations we can find
how far away they are, the galaxies,
how far between the stars, how fast they move,
how old, when they began, and in what fire.

We named the stars, we own the universe;
as we owned Eden for a little while.

.

Plum Island

Jade green waves curling
       multi-folded in unpredictable progressions, whispering
       at, toward, but never reaching, muttering
       an attack, a gift, offering
       the restless edges of profundity, teasing
       the spirit, promising
       revelation, giving
       only hope.

Gray gulls flitting like thoughts, searching
       at the depths for food, finding
       a moment's sustenance on surfaces, knowing
       of endless riches below, hungering
       for feasts of completion, having
       only the certainty of drowning.

Brown sand fixed in still waves, sliding
       imperceptibly into new shapes, resting
       as if solid, uncertainly picturing
       permanence, sculptured of pure grace, shifting
       into pleasantries, resisting
       the inevitable conclusion.

Colorless self, emptily seeking
      the gift of all this, walking
      heavily against the half-wet sand, dreaming
      the picture of eternity being here and now, accepting
      the prevarication of a durable sky, hanging
      between death and hope.

Stone blue sky, arching
      over the entirety, waiting
      to seal the covenant.

The Poppy

The poppy seed is small, a tiny speck
that lives unnoticed underneath the snow
and in the spring, unseen by hungry birds
begins its transformation to the bloom.

In Flanders Field they grow, and feed upon
the blood of those who wandered by that day
and met the bullets in their wandering path,
conjunction of the fates of men and lead.

Out of the seed will spring the memory
of those who died so young and uselessly.
Large orange blossoms, quick to fall away,
copied in plastic on memorial day,

with old men selling artificial flowers
in recognition of their finest hours.

Possums

There is a Southern creature moving in,
tempted by warming trends to travel north
to find new habitats in which to spend
its nights and days, to give its young safe birth.

It is the possum, famous Southern stew,
beloved of rural people for its taste.
However, here's no love for them, it's true.
In Vermont we let possums go to waste.

They're an invasive species, and you know
such creatures are unwelcome in this state.
We don't accept our neighbors overflow;
even the lovely loosestrife's viewed with hate.

I urge the possum, though he will not hear,
"Possum, go home. You are not welcome here."

A Prayer to the Maker

How poor the wonder of this feeble mind!
I sought to understand Your works, O God,
to know the stars; by looking down to find
the truth of little things beneath the sod

that covers natures treasures underfoot,
unfathomed distances above, below,
what flowers find when they send down their roots,
what causes distant galaxies to glow,

what are the coil-springs of the universe
that send it ever farther on its way?
Its all too large, too small, to put in verse,
all hidden things, lost in complexity.

Let me accept the earth's simplicity,
find beauty there, Your loving gift to me.

Rat

From nothing, nothing came. That's almost true.
There was a tint bit of something there
and all that is, is made from parts of that;
the universe, the people and the rat.

It's known that all of this is mostly space;
a galaxy would store inside a pin
if one could crunch its light into a place
that has no long extensions left within.

And all this glory, mystery and thrill
with which we want to live, and not let go
must fold upon itself, and finally will
be gone into that tiny space. But though

most things will be conserved and packed away
the cockroach and the rat will stay.

Red Sky at Morning

Odd, isn't it, that glories of the dawn,
the scarlet banners of the waking day,
portend a storm; that when the sun has gone
the rain will come, and turn the world to gray?

Thus nature teaches not to trust her word.
The silver lining of the darkest shroud
does not protect us from the flashing sword
of lightning falling from the threatening cloud.

"Red sky at morning;" cautionary tale
of sailors who have seen that sky at morn
an omen of a fierce and killing gale;
beware the day that was in beauty born.

It's not folk wisdom. Nature's die is cast.
Attend the signs, learn from a deadly past.

The Red-Wing

Close cousin to the Oriole, but dark;
a black-bird of the field and grassy marsh.
Oriole nests in trees close by our camp.
The Red-wing, shy, aloof, does not come near.

Surer than Robins to announce the spring,
when he arrives we know that winter's gone.
He finds his place, announces, "I am here.
All others stay away. This field is mine."

He flashes, shows his crimson epaulets.
Lord of his acre, solitary prince,
guarding his family hidden in the grass,
Tells me, "Do not come in, just quickly pass."

His simple black's deceptive. In the air
he transforms black to beauty with his flare.

Revelation

I thought that beauty was what I could see
on sunlit days, the flowers and the fields,
blue mountains rising at the valley's edge,
spindrift of grass, wind teasing at the sedge.

And what I touched, the things that I could feel,
smooth velvet cloth, and better, velvet skin,
a tender kiss that grew to passionate,
passion unlimited until passion spent,

Words, paints and music; all the artists' tries
enlightening nature for our hungry eyes;
the smell of lilacs drifting through the air,
and taste of food, an Epicurean fare.

Beauty was always there, easy to find;
"Deny the ugly, seek a spotless mind."

But then I found this grotesque piece of wood
lying on forest floor, an ugly scrap
left from a broken tree, a random fall,
all cover gone, its essence strange and wild.

It was a face of fearful agony;
a scream, a gargoyle that had always been
hidden beneath the facile beauty, seen
by shallow eyes, or eyes that would not see.

I found there is a deeper beauty here
beneath the pretty, growing out of pain,
beauty that knows it will not come again,
beauty of loss that end of life is near.

This artifact's the skeleton of truth;
there is no beauty that denies our death.

Rhythm of the Trail

I now have lost the rhythm of the trail.
The mountains rise too high; my climbing's done,
I look at valleys from the valley floor;
there is no up for me; these legs of stone.

Trees challenge me. They wave across the yard,
swaying their message clear, come dance with us.
My dance is in my head, the rhythm hard
and pulsing, rocking out my sad regrets.

The world around me dances. I am still.
The goddess takes my poetry away.
She goes with others; I am left behind.
What good is dancing that's locked in the mind?

God bless the thoughts of heaven, loss of pain,
of running with the angels, free again.

Risen Moon

The risen moon, over the eastern hills,
a harvest color now but silver soon,
cold fire of night, light on the lover's paths,
an ancient goddess, marked with mystic runes.

The goddess of the moon was chaste, untouched
by gods or men, the queen of purity,
a distant beauty, unattainable
from earth, a sign of our humility.

Then NASA came, and rockets fled the earth,
carrying capsules to our satellite,
and men walked on the moon and left their tracks
making her face the junkyard of the night.

If I look carefully, I'm sure I'll see
where men have walked, and spoiled the mystery.

The Rose

Petals compounded in a swirl of red,
a few white petals on a seaside vine,
the rose is famed for multiplicity
of size and color and utility.

It's known for those whose tomb it decorates;
the reddest rose springs up from Caesar's grave;
not contradicting it as flower of peace . . .
the grave, in history, is a peaceful place.

This is the flower of love, an honest one;
below its lovely bloom it has its sting.
Like love, true love, we know that we will need
not to hold on too tightly, or we bleed.

The queen of flowers, symbol of the heart,
queen of the courtier, and queen of thorns.

River Songs

We are tempted to treat the river.
    this lively rippling stream,
    this stream of living water,
as an entity with life and history,
    an observer that flows through time,
    a creature that has known the lives of men,
as a mind that remembers and gives to the ocean,
    ocean of enormous capacity to store information,
    whose storms are rage, whose calms are dreams of peace,
all its memories, by which the ocean also knows
    reflections of cities, recollection of floods,
    tears of drowned men, pleasures of good harvests.

There are in the river and the ocean no memories,
only various conditions of mindlessness.
The river's joy is our joy, the ocean's rage our fear.
If we sing, it is not the river's song.
    The river's noise and silences are created
    by the interaction of earth, stone and water
    tuned by gravity and friction.
The song is ours.

The River's Mouth

At the river's mouth, at the ocean's edge, the river dies,
interlacing itself with the deeper parts of the sea.
At the river's mouth, the river dies,
offering its water into the fullness of the sea
which in its final passage it creates,
which in its termination it becomes.

At the river's mouth the river appears placid
      full of years, prepared for death.
As it waits, is becomes a broad lake, a safe anchorage.
As it waits, it holds commerce, gives pleasure.
      Those who walk on its shallow marshes
      find the many inclusions of its journey
      and are interested, perhaps fascinated, by its gifts.

      Those who live at the edge of this terminal pool
      know the river's nobility, its broadest reach,
      know its final energy, its openness,
      see its last work, its final surge.

We, here, might reflect upon the river's appropriate death
        and find in it a majestic sadness.
The river, in fact, does not die.
The river's mouth is a roiling conjunction
        of moving water surging
        into the still waters of the waiting sea.
What we see, and what we do not see
are of no consequence to the river
but are of deep matter to us
who love this mindless torrent
and would celebrate its beginning, its passage, its termination,
what it has been,
what it might become.

Origins and Names

The river is born
high on a mountain;
out of a spring,
under a rock
a stream flows
the mountain's blood wells
there and from a thousand such
each like the other
trickles of water move
under dead leaves, fall
from granite ledges, join
in trail beds, seek
gullies, seek
furrows, seek
ravines, become
together a brook, a running
falling
torrent

Osceola Brook rises on Breadtray Ridge
in that fashion, and
joins with Tecumsah to begin the Mad River.
Out of the inner rim of the Wilderness come
Hellgate, Redrock, Franconia, Lincoln, Twin
into the Pemigewasset.

Beaver Brook plummets lazily
from the gothic ledges of Mossilauke,
into shattered crystal light,
rests in deep emerald pools,
bathes the standing stones,
rushes into hollows
with the voice of the wind, and
comes to the Lost River.
So is given a partial genealogy of the river
bred from well respected hills and
streams of impeccable family histories.

We might think that the names of brooks and rivers
are true, as having been given when each particular stream
came into being, and therefore we might believe
that the stream will know itself to be that which it is named.

That is of course, untrue.
We of well respected names, and
impeccable blood lines
named the streams and rivers.

And we who name streams and rivers
presume thereby to control, or
to pretend to own and control
the water and what it does.

The streams and rivers, and
the river
have origins and continuity
but have no names,
as indeed they existed
before the namers came
and will exist
when our names have disappeared.

And also, also . . .
What fool could think to own a mountain stream
swollen by melting snows in the springtime?
What fool could think to control a river?
We are allowed only to ask its favor.

The River's Passage

The river moves
past the lowland pastures, curving
among the multitudes of boulders, dividing
around the mudflat islands,
passing, passing slowly
under the bridges.
> Webster, Queen City, Tyngsboro
> Pawtucket, Hunt's Falls, Duck,
> Basiliere, Rock's Village, The Chain.
> Name the bridges, name the miles, the hours, the days
> Name the span from springs to ocean
> Name the passage.

Passing, passing gently
Through the cities
> Concord, Manchester, Nashua
> Lowell. Lawrence, Haverhill
> Newburyport
name the cities, name the miles, the hours, the days
name the journey, from hill to ocean.

What have you called it, this passage,
the rivers duration?
The day of the river, and its night?
Its sunrise, sunset? its seasons,
summer doldrums, spring floods, winter ice?

What have you called it?
Can you name the river's duration?

The river moves endlessly, like the wind.
The time of the river has no name,
not even eternity.

Through our consciousness of our time, the river
carves a passage of durable stillness.

The Presence

Between sunset and sunrise
between source and terminus
in the turn
Between the ebb and flow in the tidal zone
or behind the dam in its still moment
we come to the river
to wait with it.

Here are no shallows and backwaters
      no channels, rapids, dams
          no obscene dumps, no invading willows
             no mud bars or canals, no falls
                no sewer holes, no emerald pools.

The river in the absence of light
      dark and concealed
singing only with the voice of a whisper
      in a dead well
The river in an eternal dusk,
      murky, shadowless
the river in stasis,
      without breath.

The river is a presence
and we drift on the presence.

At Work in the Canals

The river in its middle reaches runs smoothly
wide, ponderous, powerful
       heavy with energy, swift for work.
Here it accepts the gentle direction of its banks,
and having collected the outpourings of
the Winnipisaukee and
the Nashua,
and having collected the excesses of
the hillside farms and towns
it accepts also the hindrance of the dams,
rises to an appropriate height
and waits.

The river is very still
at the Pawtucket dam,
surface unrippled, motion tamed,
slave river, chained for the work of men
by the work of men;
tractable river, gentle river,
disciplined
quiet
waiting
sullen static river,
being not a river not in motion.

We have built large ditches
and cleverly aligned and graded them
to channel our impounded waters
through certain places and machines
to produce certain motions.

Release the river;
mill wheels turn and people work and are clothed.

Release the river
into the races;
generators spin, factories assemble and lamps burn.

Release the river
into the locks;
canals fill, barges rise and fall and commerce lives.

The river is our tool;
release the river,
technology triumphs.

Clearly, the river, being mindless
cares nothing for dams or not dams.
We feel the tension of blocked energy
        and celebrate the success of engineering.

We feel sadness at movement stilled
        and joy in freedom reestablished.
We accept the myth of the river's tractability
And wait for the flood that will destroy that myth.

The River at Sunrise

There is at the Groveland crossing
a modest bridge, the Bates,
useful for cars, trucks not too large,
bicycles, walkers, joggers, dogs,
fisherboys, snigglers,
gangs of girls laughing to the plaza,
and all manner of people
and machines not here noted, but ordinary.

From this bridge, in summer looking east
in the early morning dark, when most of the above
are sleeping, and the pigeons,
still undisturbed,
accompany the ending night
with their soft invisible cluckings,
we observe the sunrise on the river
as on a great lake.

On days
when the clouds, that aligned themselves,
radiating precisely outward
from the rising point
arranged to assist the sun
announce the day,
have again become disorderly;
and
when the rose light
that spiraled out in folded blazes
has reached the west and faded,

when the sun, now colorless,
has shown its white hot center
to a pale sky,
and day has now begun,

we remember that the movements of color
above the river were of the river also,
that the river seemed the other half of the sky,
that for a brief moment it was not the river
but something more, or less.

But there are times at sunrise
when the sun is less demanding,
when the river, independent of the sky
becomes a white lake,
caught between still shadowy lines of trees
from which black cormorants hunt,
and times when the sun,
in a playful, waking dance
skips light across the river
as we might, when childish, skip stones
across a pond.
We remember then
that the river is not a mirror
but a deep, moving pool
in which there is much life
and much color
beyond the transient decorations
of a rising sun.

Hard Times on the River

We have seen the river in flood,
given more than it can hold
it simply expands into the lowlands
for a time.

Unfortunate, we who felt safe
in the myth of our own strength.
The river, like the wind,
goes where its necessity commands.

We have seen the river in drought,
given less than it can contain,
its bed becomes dry and
checks
into the patterns of the desert.
Its base rock, sharp ridged, bares itself
and its bottom becomes a revelation of tires,
        boats, bedsprings, beer cans and washing machines
among the clumps of avaricious willows.
We have also seen the river return.

Terminal Marsh

On slow days we have come to Plum Island
at the time of low tide
to search the marshes for strange and wonderful things.
What we have found is, for the most part,
crafted wood, planks of various lengths,
      smooth, sodden,
      with rounded edges and
      strongly raised grain,
      uniformly gray.

We have imagined,
      for we will have our wonder
      even in a crafted board,
that this is a piece of wood
hand-planed by some colonial carpenter
and now discarded, some centuries later,
by a careless laborer engaged
in the clearance of slums.

So much, we think, for the history of a people.

Early in the education of our children
the conscientious teacher of simple science
informs the class of the water cycle:
that the sun's heat causes vapor to rise from the ocean,
that the clouds form and are moved
by winds aloft back to the land,
shifting in large masses, until,
lifted into cool space by rising air,
water condenses and falls to the hills
to create, again, the river,
to come again to the sea.

What the teacher may not tell
is of the endlessness of water
and of the river's endless necessity
to flow and merge,
to become, to cease,
and be again,
and of its movement
as it drains and washes the land
and carries our history
into the terminal marsh.

Season's Songs

There are the songs of Springtime, when the winds
are soft, and gentle rains of April fall;
cantatas to the waking flowers, praise
to all the seeds that keep our hopes alive.

The songs of summer, hot and dry, will sweep
atonal, fierce across the fields of hay,
and grace notes to the chicory and ferns
will rise above the unmelodic lines.

The chants of autumn, stately arias
to fading asters and to falling leaves,
we sing in longing tones, a dying fall
with no crescendos; voices fade away.

And then in winter, crystal notes arise;
continuo of life, to frozen skies.

Seed Time

You would not know, to see the snow-filled fields
that they are rich with life, and thawing yields
forests of grass that grow from dormant roots
and resting seeds, the Mother's waiting fruits.

Today, the snow-goose landing place is bare,
flocks stopping, long delayed, would perish there.
The stones that were in summer gray and green
are blackened now in winter's lightless scene.

But death has lost its sting, the End its power,
its work assigned precisely for this hour;
to harden winter seeds and tender shoots
and give a resting time to living roots.

Our Mother does not die, She only rests.
Her children wait the freshening of her breasts.

September Prayer

God grant, this year, no russet winds
no frost fields, no smoke filled days,
no chilled September mornings.
Let there be no valleys gold
under red and gold mountains.
And let there be no clean trails
for walking on high ridges;
may there be no shocks of corn
nor pumpkins nestled in the rustling blades
Cover, God, the bright cold star-filled night
with your mercy's clouds;
send winter quickly.
I am too frail a shell this year, O God,
from all your love
to bear the joy of autumn.

The Seven Wonders of the Little World

Yes, there are angels still beneath the stones
that hide the little wonders from our eyes.
We see the miracles of mountains, oceans, stars;
we know the demons who, unseen,
can confiscate our glasses and our keys. The artist does not see
    the thing,
she sees the light that flows between,
and paints invisibilities that touch the soul.

But miracles are built on miracles beneath,
and even smaller miracles can be found.
Look, friends!
There is no place that is not wonder-filled,
that does not hold a womb of glory;
how can we jaded be?
With every breath we breathe a bit of air
that Moses breathed,
and share the molecules of Adam and of Gabriel.

Glory be to God for little things;
the gladiator bee that stings,
the hummingbird with ever moving wings,
the first faint smell of spring that brings
the end of winter.

I count the seven wonders of the little world,
the hidden world that waiting to be found.

Look at the hummingbird that never rests,
having the air its only nest,
flitting with ever moving wings,
seen, then unseen, feeding on tiny drops
of sweetness from the flowers breast.

Consider the earthworm, perfect beast,
hermaphroditic, loving in simple unity,
living in perfect harmony with its universe.
Its food and excrement both are sweet;
in passing through it fills its destiny,
and mindless nourishes the plants and us.

What shall we say of fruit flies,
Drosophila melanogaster,
on whose last name a horde could perch uncrowded?
Let one ripe peach rest on your window sill
and fruit flies will appear, a living proof
of the old alchemists discovery;
life can arise spontaneously, and will;
life out of death, a tiny overwhelming truth.

You've surely seen the flea, but did you know
it holds the long-jump record of the world?
A flea can jump from dog to dog
a thousand times its length away,
and fleas are brilliant, can be taught
to entertain the crowds as well as any elephant.

Let your minds descend into the stuff
of which the galaxies are made.
The single atom is a tiny sun with planets in its grasp,
there and not there, in Heisenberg uncertainty,
unseen forever, vital mystery.

And smaller yet, child of the atom.
exists the gamma ray, weak emanation of the sun.
But let two galaxies collide, or suns collapse
and gamma rays, together, flash a light
so very brief and brighter than a thousand suns.

The poet saw the cosmos in a grain of sand.
The poet saw,
indeed,
better than he knew.
With all its empty space removed,
all grains of sand, all stars, all suns, all earths
fit in that grain and did, and will again.

There gratitude enough for mighty things;
poems at sunrise, songs in the setting sun.
The poet sings the star-filled universe,
mountains and rivers, valleys, eagles wings;
all make the spirit soar.

So praise the cosmic sight,
and God, who makes the day and night,
but praise, also, the little things
from which true wonder springs.

The Shape of Darkness

What is the shape of darkness? It was there
before creation when the stygian night
was not yet made, not only lacking light;
the dark was of itself, a nothing, clear.

We cannot know true darkness on the earth.
Light from the stars sift through the deepest clouds,
and even in eclipse the sun is bright;
some say in death light shines within the shrouds.

Go to the deepest caverns of the mind.
Even there a glimpse of hope breaks through the shell
of hopelessness, and those who search can find
a single ray to lead it from its hell.

Since light began, eternally it shone;
True darkness, uncreated, ever gone.

Sit Back and Enjoy

When was the last time you took thought
to create planets, suns and moons and stars?
To set in motion solar winds, or more
set off enormous bangs from lots of stuff

that wasn't even there seconds before,
created space and time from that great well
of nothingness. Made mass and energy
in proper balance through the whole machine?

You never did. Not your responsibility.
Whoever did it did not ask for you
to mess about where you can never go,
wandering space, confusing Heaven's flow.

What you did get . . . He gave you Eden's gift.
Sit back, enjoy while there's some time left.

Snowfall

We waited in November's frozen haze,
all autumn colors gone, leaves only brown;
the season's lowest point, the devil's crown
of boredom set upon the lifeless days.

Then in a night, the snow began to come,
soft crystals drifting slowly to the ground,
covering sodden leaves, and all around
prepared earth's canvas for the rising sun.

And with the snow, the wind brought out its brush,
shaded the drifts and contours of the fields,
revealed new shapes in every stone and tree,
a Christmas print in simple clarity.

And for a time, in trackless virgin snow
we looked in wonder at the morning's glow.

Some Scattered Comments on the Universe

Parallel Universes

A universe is a universe
sprung from another universe
which in turn began
in the explosion of a tiny piece
of some other field
of rapidly expanding gases.

Alas, which is worse;
a single universe to understand
or all the curses possible
in an infinity of universes
with all the complications
thereunto appertaining?

For now, I'll settle for just one;
one earth, one sun, and one dark sky
on which to display the stars
and the moon and the fireflies.
That will do for now.

As for the other,
we'll see.

Caution

Look. Look all you want, but do not touch
the sun, the moon, the planets or the stars.
Your touch will spoil the scene,
     corrode the universe, weaken delicate energies.
This was not made for your amusement.

Look, look at the stars,
     those fiercely burning balls of gases,
     hot and tenuous, not eternal.
Let them float freely, as they are.

Look, and do not touch.
You are to be everlasting voyeurs,
     by time's demand you are in isolation.
     Do not try to spoil the stars.
     They do not need your desolation.

Make all the explanations that you need;
     curtains of dark matter,
     galactic lenses bending light,
     black holes with draculaic appetites,
     anti-matter lurking in musty hollows between the stars.
Draw diagrams, experiment in thought.

Your brilliant minds have leave to burn the earth,
     even, perhaps, your sun.

But that is all. When you are done
make sure your plague of knowledge
has done no further harm.

Look, lust for, envy the dark abyss of space,
but do not touch.

Bones

The stuff of which my bones are made
was first made in a star.

I am assured of this by science,
and have no cause to doubt.

I love the hope this gives,
that when my time is done
on this fair place,
I will burn out, as that star did,
blazing into eternal silence.

Cometology

We are:
ice balls and cosmic dirt,
wandering back and forth
among the planets and the asteroids.

We did not shape the universe.
Mostly trash, we carry information
in small and steady presentations.
We are the postmen of the system,
trapped forever in our wells of gravity,
always returning, lovely for a while in the black sky,
but in the cosmic population, insignificant.

But, be careful. Don't get in our way.
One of our sisters killed off the dinosaurs.

Query

I look at the night sky
on those rare occasions, in Vermont
when one can see the stars
and think I know
as much as all the astronomers
who've ever done the same,
even the ones with telescopes.

We're all voyeurs,
        some as scientists,
        some as poets.

Together, someday, we will explain it all.

Then, what will we do in our spare time?

Necrocosmology

When will we die?
Not noticeably soon.
Our heartbeats match the resonances
of the black hole's thrumming.

Our birthday celebrations
      are light years apart.

We are, in mythic terms, immortal
      as a group.

Yet even we can hear
time's winged chariots
drawing near.

Eternity for the Blessed

Imagine
Time without motion
Eternity

But time is well defined by change
       something must move
       and move in well marked space

Eternity is the death of time
       and in eternity, therefore,
nothing moves

Imagine
       angels and the redeemed
       around the throne of God
       singing His praises,
       but motionless, mouths open,
blissful faces

Soundless for eternity.

No Consolation There

They're aging;
the stars that started their journeys
with such happy, lilting energies,
believing they would never die,
are dying.

If we could talk
I'd tell them all
that aging is a common ill
alike for us and for the galaxies
and in the end
we'll all be still.

Spring Begins

When, do you think, begin the springtime hours?
When the warm breeze of April brings the flowers?
When crocus blooms defiant in the snow?
When pheromones rise up, and maidens glow?

That evidence is good; life has begun
that journey to the summer and the fall
that blesses life beneath the father sun,
that gives us joy even though the time is small.

I take a view contrary to the rest.
I think that spring begins at winter solstice.
I see the coming light when in the west
I see the rising sun shorten the dark.

We do not need to wait for daffodils;
just mark the sunrise on your windowsills.

Spring Sonnet

What is this feeling that we have for Spring
after the long gestation in the bleak
cold womb of winter, worlds unseen,
songs left unsung, life muffled by the snow?

"Ah, glorious spring!" I know that that is trite
but truth can bear repeating times again.
Spring is the rising sun that ends the dark,
after the night of winter, and the rain.

Now if the clouds will come, and sure they will,
they'll bring the rains of April, and the flowers
will bloom, the sparkling daffodil throw back
the sunlight, until all the earth is filled

with light, and warmth, and lovely growing things
and I will say again "Ah, glorious spring!"

Stars

Small points of light from here, but furnaces
raging in place, place never still; they flee
that single blast that once began in space,
sweeping in silence through eternity.

Or maybe not. The endlessness we scan
(we've scanned it only for a little while)
may be a temporary state for man,
observing 'til observing's out of style.

It does not matter where they are, how grand.
The stars amuse us now, even inspire,
but not to glory; our attention span,
limits our vision, turns us from the fire.

The stars are there forever in their flight.
It's we who vanish in the passing night.

Summer Wine

Now we have drunk the last of summer's wine.
The locust snows begin, the maple leaves
have carpeted the woodland trails, entwine
the colors radiant in autumn's end.

It is the terminus of summer's might,
the fading joy of all that summer was,
a sadness at the dying of the light
at winter's unforgiving reign of tears.

I must confess that swiftly passing years
leave me with empty seasons that I've lost.
I cannot reconcile recurring tears
with deeper gladness that we shared the most.

Time, in its mindless progress leaves behind
sweet passions that we now shall never find.

The Sun Blesses The Earth

Sweet sun, whose soft radiance comes liltingly
        through bare and waiting branches,
bring your unsteady warmth to the cold winds of spring.
Tempt out the tiny plants, which first must live in trust
        before they live in certainty
and bless them against the iron hard memory of winter's end.

Fierce sun, whose raging energy brings into final form
        the summer's leaf and flower,
give to the plants their shape and strength,
call forth the seemingly dead seed of life ongoing,
and bless the Mother in her green fruition.

Strong sun, to whom all water will return,
        relentless creator of the desert,
as days move toward the blazing death of autumn,
rest on the restless, shifting leaves; finish life
and bless the earth with silence.

Ancient sun, resting and giving rest in these late days
        as earth returns to cold;
small and distant sun, now in the gray well if winter,
as night begins, let death begin,
and bless the earth with hope.

Sundial, Sometimes

The night is long in winter, and the day
is often leaden, with a threat of snow;
seamless progression of the black to gray,
the dials unlit, and time is passing slow.

These timeless days, when boredom reigns supreme
and sundials wait a signal from the sun;
joyless my thoughts, I wander in a dream
of absent poetry, songs left unsung.

But let the sun break through, and all is well;
colors return, all things become themselves.
Sun's shadows strike the hours, begin to tell
the glowing times, and darkness seems to leave.

The sun's my clock, and when the god ascends
I know that time exists, will never end.

Sun Prisoned by Clouds

Must I sit helpless while the winter sun
is locked, unjustly, in a cloudy cell?
Shall I let mists take precedence while he
must languish, powerless to make his show,

dressed in his royal robes, in majesty,
to light his waiting earth, denying life?
What sorrow must I feel, what dark accept
when darkness should be day, our sun should shine?

Oh, I would mount my horse, and charge the sky,
sword flashing, rip the sullen clouds apart,
set free the morning light and loose his gift
to bless his world, to let us see again.

No, I must wait; let nature its course,
but still I cry, "My kingdom for a horse!"

The Surf is Raging

From halfway round the world, called by the moon,
surf rages wildly at the ocean's edge,
the crashing waves seem to desire to take
the land back to their heart, to cover all.

Born in the hills, I had not seen the sea
until I stood at this incoming tide,
and saw the power, the overwhelming surge,
lost from the safety of my mountain home.

The ocean wants the hills, wants to include
all that they are in all the ocean is,
bring up the valleys, wash the mountains low
'til all's a level plain, time at an end.

And if the ocean's wish is then fulfilled,
All will be one, and all of nature stilled.

Sysiphus on Mount Washington

Here child, first timer,
resting on your lichened seat,
youth filled, quick to recover;
you, sweet athlete, breathing so powerfully,
while you rest, include me in your view.
I too am landscape, though I move.

Why do you climb this sweet and holy hill?
The sudden opening of clouds at trails end?
To prove your strength? Because it's there?
To end some adolescent dream?
Reasons of innocence, capable of conclusion.

I have another reason, for myself,
brief and to the point; necessity.
A man might climb because he has no choice.
His life might be constrained,
Not between birth and death,
But between base and summit,
Between beginning and never ending,
as mine is.

What do you see? You think me old, sweet child?
Your thought's bounds will not contain my age.
You, caught between some common acts,
whose life is in obliging step with the progressing hours,
will never comprehend the ages I've spent here,
nor will you ever, with that trembling mind
know mine, whose father was the master of the winds;
this mind, which tricked the gods and almost, almost won.

Oh, I am weird to you, and all you see
set on these trails, this old and lumpish flesh,
this boulder I must ever lift and push
and ever see slip back, past the ravines,
down winter paths and head walls . . .
All you see is a mad and aged man.
This much I'll tell you; try to take it in.
You see the ancient enemy of the gods,
honored and cursed by this task on this hill.

Well . . . do not fear this garrulous old man.
My rage is not for you;
I speak to you because I found you here.
My hatred is for those who can no longer listen,
for those who gave me this eternal drudgery
and ran to the delicious silence of their graves.
For them I shall forever rage;
forever, or I until I come upon
that moment of eternal balance
when I remain in stillness at the top.

All you see is a mad and aged man,
climbing this root-ribbed rock-bound lump of earth
which has been squatting almost endlessly.
You, innocent child, who praise this lovely hill,
and never knew the devious gods who piled it here
for me and me alone.
You climb! Your puny sweat erodes no lasting mark.
I have been given eternity to wear it down,
and wear it down I will!

I too have loved these hills.
All I see I desire to become,
to let my spirit fly in winds across the wilderness,
to bring it back entire,
to stretch myself into the valleys, crash across summits
until I join the ocean at its edge.

Someday I will dance across these hills,
as summer dances in her rising light . . .
a touch, a touch, a fleeting touch
feet dusting gently past the cairns,
hills rising up to meet my whispering steps.

Not yet, not yet.
For now I'll drag this flesh across
these finger tearing granite prison walls
to please Olympian wardens
who may have forgot the sentence.

That is my question, child of man:
I think the old gods live.
I know they live in this undying mind
and so they live among these hills.
They live in my strength and in my rage,
cold gods, relentless and alive in me.
But if their only dwelling place is here,
what gods will set me free?

A Tree Dies

The stately elm, fanned to the setting sun,
with lacy foliage thin, seemed in distress.
An elm, she said, should have more greenery,
There's something wrong with it. I cannot guess

what it could be. It has been there for years,
standing alone to guard the farmer's road.
Maybe a worm has eaten in below
and kept the earth from letting in its food,

Or maybe dust has gotten on its leaves
and blocked the sun's life-giving energy
or some dark canker in its heartwood lies
and says you have no further time to be.

I think she's tired of standing there alone.
She has no joy with all her sisters gone.

A Cosmic Question

With simple calculations we can find
how far away they are, the stars,
how far between them, this collection
of the celestial fireflies, St. Elmo's fires,
swamp gases burning in the firmament.

And knowing distances, and spectral shifts,
we know how far they've traveled,
when the journey started, or if they're there at all.

We know the stuff of cinders left when one star died
in a funeral pyre brighter than a galaxy,
only for a day.

We know their names. We should; we christened them.

And since we acted thus, do we now own the universe
as we once possessed Eden?

To a Vermont Winter

The sun appeared today, at least I think
it is the sun, remembered from the fall
before that season died in winter's pall
and left us watching Vermont's beauty sink

into almost eternal dim-lit days
and rain and snow and sleet begin to drop
in drear anticipation, when the tops
of mountains disappear, when we can't raise

a smile, and sundials lose efficiency
since only shadows cannot tell the time
and the sole decoration's frosty rime
growing from twigs on leafless, barren trees.

I think if there's a hell (there's not, I pray!)
the flames will burn in sooty black and gray.

Waking

Clear sky and sunrise
over eastern mountains.
A well lit silence.

Waiting Time

May in Vermont was not as nasty as April.
Daffodils came from frozen ground
and lilacs bloomed.
Juices flowed,
though the sap had finished running.
Old men, slower than maple syrup,
remembered and hoped.
That winter was chilly, with
plenty of snow for a change,
though it came late,
just in time for spring skiing.
The people from Connecticut
slid down the hills, breaking their butts
from time to time.I did not know ice had undone so many.
Summer was a surprise!
Two feet of snow in June
racing across Mt. Dick and Whiteface
raising spindrift, then whitecaps,
then great waves across Champlain.
That summer I skied, first and last time.
My instructor, in her middle years,
offered to carry my skis down to the lodge.
The aging population watched TV
and spent the winter in Florida.

Winter Demons

Snake Mountain, to the east, is like a cloud
floating above the Dead Creek's frozen swamp,
a looming, solid mist caught in the shroud
that rises in cool autumn's morning damp

a backdrop to the trees that sway against
a sullen sky, moving to sluggish winds,
a crimson sunrise, one of nature's hints
to sailors, rain will fall before day's end.

Why not complain? I've seen her better times.
This was a glorious scene and still might be.
I can't afford to go to warmer climes.
Must I accept this everlasting gray?

A dull-demeanored world at every hand.
The winter demons lurk to stew the land

The Winter Earth

The winter earth's reflected in the sky;
gray hills, gray trees trapped in the black-walled snow.
The world is small, closed to my spirits flow;
the clouds are close, birds have no space to fly.

My soul, sleep-walking, wanders round about
this evening darkness in the midst of day
when even the dim sun has gone away.
What can be clear; what can be safe from doubt?

What is the source of knowledge, where to find;
when darkness limits day, denies the bright
vision that breaks out when the rising light
reveals earth's beauty and renews my mind?

My laggard brain's still sleeping, and the flight
of my soul's fancy can't escape the night.

Winter in Vermont

I've always been a stranger here.
I fell into Vermont by wedding bells,
and found a mystery in this green land:
it's truly hard to tell the seasons well apart;
when summer comes,
or when the autumn starts.

Sometimes it's warm in winter;
but though an early crocus bloom,
it often dies in deeper snow;
or Lake Champlain is frozen in July,
or in autumn blooms again the rose.

The season's limits, as you see, are iffy,
but there's one sign that tells you in a jiffy
when winter comes and goes.

Vermont is justly famous for its cows,
and all the bovine products
of the highest quality; butter, milk and cheese,
and less often mentioned, still of these,

Manure.

Stored in large tanks in winter
to protect the Lake,
to insure its unphosphoric quality,
but loosed across the roads and rich gray fields
in which the silage grows,

in springtime
and in summer
and in fall.

This fact defines one season very well.
A Vermont winter
is the season when it doesn't smell.

What Color is the Sun?

A what color is the sun? It shimmers in
the various colors of the heavens' fires,
but at the summers end the colors fade.
I see the autumn's sadness in the sun.

What color is the sun? I've seen it red,
coming around the corners of the world,
lying like blood on autumn's fallen leaves,
waking the birds, closing the door on night.

What color is the sun? I've seen it white,
motionless, pale in autumn's dying light,
lifeless at noon, portending winter's storms,
lighting the world with ashen radiance.

What color is the sun? I've seen it gold,
set in the fading sky to close the day,
all golden in the autumn's golden dusk,
a final blaze before the coming dark.

I see the autumn's sadness in the sun,
waking the birds, closing the door on night,
lighting the world with ashen radiance,
a final blaze before the coming dark.

What Do We Know?

What do we know in the springtime
when the world is new and green,
and the crocus blooms through the dusty snow
and the east wind blows from the sea?

This we know in the springtime
when we hear the new lambs call,
that flowers will bloom forever,
and life is long and sweet.

What do we know in the summer
when the world is deep and rich,
and chicory blooms by the ragged roads
and the south wind blows from the fields?

This we know in the summer,
when clover's alive with bees,
in the August light on the eastern hills
that life is hot and sweet.

What do we know in the autumn
when the world is slow and brown,
and the last fern blooms near the dusty stone
and the west wind blows from the hills?

This we know in the autumn
when the leaves are a mist if gold,
in the resting woods, in the dying woods
that life is old and sweet.

What do we know in the winter
when the world is white and chilled,
and nothing blooms by the frozen pond
and the north wind blows from the stars?

This we know in the winter,
when the snow drifts down from the pines
in the evening light, when the light is gone,
that life is cold, and sweet.